Through the Window of My Heart

Spiritual Poetry

Judy Johnson
Bless you as you
carry on His work.

Helen Kuester

By Helen Kuester

PUBLISH AMERICA

PublishAmerica
Baltimore

12-2007

First printing

At the specific preference of the author, PublishAmerica allowed this work to remain exactly as the author intended, verbatim, without editorial input.

ISBN: 1-4241-9711-2
PUBLISHED BY PUBLISHAMERICA, LLLP
www.publishamerica.com
Baltimore

Printed in the United States of America

I wish to dedicate this God-inspired book to my family and especially my granddaughter, Stacie Witschorik. She initiated the process and carried it to completion. Without her faith in God, this book would not have been accomplished.

Thus says the Lord,
the God of Israel:
Write all the words
that I have spoken to you
in a book.

Jeremiah 30:2

Table of Contents

Through the Window
of My Heart

Spiritual Poetry

ACCEPTANCE

We wonder when a loved one leaves
for the eternal home.
We feel we need to keep them here,
instead they're gone alone.

But this morning as I pondered,
how He chooses those He calls,
I realized His way, as always,
keeps us from all pit falls.

If we were to choose who dies
what a dilemma that would be.
For we could never give up those
who are loved by you and me.

So once again our Savior
displays His perfect plan.
He calls us on the journey home
to the promised land.

Now, we can't see the reason,
as we try to understand.
But we know they're in His presence,
and we know He holds our hand.

BIBLE STUDY BLESSING

Thank you Lord for bringing us
these precious folks tonight.
They're here to read the Bible
and live their lives aright.

I said I was too tired Lord,
you said, "Let's wait and see,"
and then you gave me rest and peace
then renewed my energy.

And now I feel real joy again,
excitement in the Lord.
You tossed my tired feelings out
and filled me with your word.

BLESSINGS

Remind me Lord
to be sweet and good,
to say only the things
that you tell me I should.

When I start to feel
that things aren't fair,
help me to see
that it gets me no where.

As I read your words
in your Holy Book,
my eyes find your truth
wherever I look.

Your teaching is perfect
and it's leading me on—
pointing out truths
and making me strong.

I thank you Heavenly Father
for everything you do.
Teaching us just how to live
so we can live for you.

SUMMER RAIN

God sends the flowers needed rain
when they wilt and stoop so low.
Then as a miracle they rise
to stand erect and show
their new found beauty sent by God,
through moisture from above.
For we who give our every care,
He sends His strength and love.

Now the soft summer rain
falls gently down
and touches the flowers with dew.
Oh, we thank you God
for knowing our needs
and bringing us back to you.

In all our lives some rain must fall.
The clouds are gray above,
then suddenly the sun shines through
with the warmth of the Father's love.
We are His flowers trying to bloom,
out in the world we pale,
but we always know as we trust in God,
that His love will never fail.

In His Steps

Oh let me walk as Jesus walked
along the roads and paths of strife,
and as I walk as Jesus walked,
oh, take my hand and lead my life.

Help me to daily follow Him
up to the home, His home on high.
Teach me to guide, and teach as well
our fellowmen, lest some may die.

I'll thank you Jesus all the way
as Thy sweet praises do I sing,
and knowing well, Thy spirits here
to lift these praises to the King.

THE GIFT

I've been blessed with many friends,
the best that they can be.
For the tie that binds us together,
also sets us free.

The Lord is the common thread,
that intertwines us all.
For He gives love and truth and hope,
that lifts us should we fall.

Now friendship is a special gift,
it's given freely from above.
You know it doesn't cost a cent
and comes through Jesus, by His love.

LITANY OF PRAISE

Lord, lead my thoughts all through this day.
Help me to walk in your sweet way.
As you listen to my prayerful thoughts,
I realize my sin you've bought.
As I lift my hands in praise,
I feel your love and peaceful grace,
and I breathe, thank you Lord!

HIS PEACE

Do you ever long for morning
in the middle of the night?
Do you have that restless feeling
wishing for the early light?

Do you toss and turn with anxious thoughts
that just won't go away?
Then, turn your mind to Jesus
as you fold your hands and pray.

You'll soon feel the sweet surrender
just relax and go to sleep,
with the Holy Spirit's comfort
sending angels' watch to keep.

God bless you with peace.

PARALLEL

The rain, falling softly
was announced by thunder.
A bold display of wrath
dazzled the western sky.

In retrospect,
a much-needed rain fell,
chilling the earth
preparing it for winter—a quiet time.

As in our lives
we are prepared for life beyond,
where thunder and storms
in our lives will not be,
where only love and peace will reign.

TRANSPARENCY

To God we are a vessel of clear glass,
for He can look at our souls
and see our inner-self.
Let us be honest with self,
accept the way of the Lord
and be aware of salvation.

Let us polish this vessel,
with the cloth of righteousness,
until sparkles of love
cast God's inner glow on others,
that they too, by God's grace,
through the Holy Spirit,
will also accept and receive joy.

(see 2 Corinthians 4:7)

OUR LIFETIME

Spring is a new beginning,
not unlike our lives
that from birth need nourishment.
Then growth happens
and springs forth with hope and expectancy.

Then there's our years of summer,
sunny days and warm nights
when we are young and strong.
We revel in our time to work and grow.

I realized in the fall of my life
as I see the leaves fall from the trees
leaving trees still alive,
but lacking in beauty
where the word "fall" comes from.

Winter settles into our region—it's relentless.
As in our lives,
with no turning back,
we look back on our life in that past,
as we are reminded
and get used to, impending death.

But for Christians, it doesn't end in death.
For this is our hope for the future,
to meet our Savior and live eternally with joy,
where there are no seasons,
only peace and love will prevail.

CONVERSATION

Lord we ask so much of you
such as healing for a friend,
to keep things running smoothly,
you are the great I AM!

I appreciate your goodness
filled with love and happiness,
leading us down pathways
never faltering with love.

You give us faith and peaceful rest,
you tell us not to doubt,
you straighten all my messes,
and soon the sun bursts out.

Sometimes when roads are rocky
and we have to catch our breath,
then we stop and lean on Jesus,
looking forward to His rest.

STRENGTH

Our strength is sent from the Lord you know,
we have no abilities except through Him.
Whenever the winds of trouble may blow,
there's no need to worry if we trust in Him.

Our friendship grows stronger day by day,
as we accept Him more.
He waits for us til we open to Him.,
yes, He knocks on every heart's door.

Invite Him in, He loves us so,
give Him the chance to show,
when you let the Lord come
and live in your heart,
all that is good will grow.

DEAR FATHER

I paused to thank and pray today
for all the blessings sent my way—
my loving friends and family too,
the way you've taught me to "make do".

As I think about the answers
to prayers I sent your way,
how you sent your Son from glory,
to lift my sins, their price to pay.

How you fill my head with reason
showing clearly what to do,
how I love you Heavenly Father,
always, I depend on you.

DAY BREAK

Early morning rising
is a challenge every day.
But when we learn to do it,
it seems the better way.

We get to see the sunrise,
more of the tasks get done.
there's more precious time,
to pray for everyone.

Now every day's a blessing.
Life's road we all must trod.
It's a beautiful safe highway,
when we give our lives to God.

THANK YOU

Lord we lean on you so totally
to guide our life.
We thank you for the confidence you give
whenever there is strife.

We bless your name in pride
in knowing you,
and praise with absolute,
your love, forever true.

We know the joy we feel
does come from you,
and that the Holy Spirit
in every aspect of our lives,
will see us through.

CHEERFUL GIVING

I expect of you your all,
not resting, but doing.
Accomplishing what you set out
and need to do is the only way to
achieve success in your life.
Your promises are of extreme
importance you know.

REQUEST

What can I do for you Father?
What can I do today?
I'll tell you what my daughter,
right now, kneel down and pray.

Now that I prayed dear Father
and rekindled my life for you,
give me the tasks that need doing,
with your help I will carry them through.

Break down the wall of sadness.
Give love to all you meet.
Put joy inside where darkness hides.
I'll bring victory and chase out defeat.

THE SEASONS OF OUR LIFE

One by one the dear old friends
slip quietly away,
and the pastor says, "We'll meet again"
as the people sadly pray.

We've lost so many "dear old friends"
as the leaves fall from the trees,
so the seasons of our life go on
as we flutter like the leaves.

When God in His mercy calls us home
what joy will fill our soul,
but we leave behind the loved ones
to hear the church bells toll.

Then they too will hear the promise
and hear the Pastor say,
"Take heart, believe, beloved,
you'll meet again some day."

HE SETS OUR PATHS STRAIGHT

When we say, "Oh Lord, what can we do?
We're willing, but there's nothing for you
that we can start and do today."
He sends the work and right away.

A neighbor calls or some dear friend,
just needing a listening ear to bend.
An errand run, a steadying arm,
a little child to keep from harm.
There's always plenty we can do.
If we ask the Lord, there's work for you.

JOY

Those that haven't found it
are afraid they will lose it.
Those that have, know,
and are never afraid again.

Where there is faith
there is also contentment
in the soul.

LOVE

To love someone is to know their inner-self,
to willingly perceive the needs of others.
Acting unselfishly on their behalf and
remembering always,
lest we feel a mite self-righteous,
That we who give gains more.

FAITH

It doesn't matter where we are
or if we're far apart,
what matters most of all
is Jesus in our hearts.

Though distance separates us
and we can't see or touch,
the love of Jesus keeps us close
and nothing means so much.

For we are in His circle,
His arms enfold with love,
Oh the goodness of His mercy,
the abundance of His dove*.

Our dependence just grows stronger
as we journey on each day,
listening for His precious guidance
as with thankful hearts we pray.

*Holy Spirit

FORGIVENESS

The people mourned for Moses,
they thought they couldn't go on.
But God in His mercy led them,
and through Him were made strong.

It's the same in our life today, friends,
when we look back on all our strife
and remember sadness instead of joy,
There's no room for growth in life.

So forget the wrongs done to us,
and tell the devil to flee.
Remember, forgive and pray for our foes,
Christ died for you and me!

THE COMFORTER

Wherever we are,
wherever we go,
the Lord keeps showing
He loves us so.
He takes our stresses
and blows them away,
He puts the sunshine
back in our day.
His mercy is endless,
His grace covers our sin,
so open your heart's door,
and let Him come in.

MORE BLESSINGS

There'll be blessing beyond measure
when you have more of Me in your life.
It's the souls of the righteous I treasure
when they ask I will give them new life.

It'll be easier to be understanding
when people turn away,
from truth of the gospel you share,
but the seed will grow when it's planted,
with My love beyond compare.

Now don't be afraid to go forward
bringing the lost to Me,
I'll open My arms and enfold them
and whisper, "My child, I love thee".

ASSURANCE

You have trusted
and have found
I truly am your provider.

You have been anxious
on the highways
and I have shown
I am your protector.

You've had parental concern
and prayed against Satan's wiles.
But I have turned lives around.
I am God and I break habits.

Hearts have been broken.
I have healed them.
Through prayer and supplication
I can do all things.

I AM the great I AM.

His Promise

None of us are worthy
to come before the Lord.
Not one more worthy than others
and yet we're still adored.

Our heavenly Father loves us.
He wants us for His own.
Give Him a chance to prove His truth
and make His wishes known.

If we but turn our minds from Him
and look the other way,
satan gladly fills our heads
with ridiculous things to say.

So keep your eyes on Jesus,
He'll help you into joy.
Then all your thoughts and things you do
shall then His will employ.

TIME

My time is delegated to me by the Lord,
to spend it as I feel led to do,
not as others see fit for me
to accomplish their needs.
I must gaze only on Jesus
and ask Him for the beneficial strength
that only He can give
through the Holy Spirit
and the abilities to guide my life
according to His desires.

Prayer for Healing

Father, I beseech you.
Help me as I plead.
Send your Holy Spirit,
grant me what I need.

What I need is healing.
What I need is love.
Send your Holy Spirit,
cleansing from above.

Help me, give me courage
as I go on through
the testing I need to have,
I put all my faith in you.

How Are We Strengthened

Strength through adversities,
strength from above,
strength as we need it,
sent through His love.

For this a promise
He gave long ago,
as He came to save us,
He'll never let go.

So let's thank our Savior,
give Him our praise,
for all that is needed,
is His fond embrace.

How Beautiful

How beautiful are your ways Lord,
how tender is your care.
How you move others and ourselves,
to create your presence here.

PRAISE

Seek Me in all things.
I will show the way that is good.
Praise is sweet to my ears,
and I will pour out blessings innumerable!

REDEMPTION

Oh Lord how wonderful are your ways,
you make our lives complete.
And when we fall and from you stray,
you bring us back, to kneel at your feet.

We know that comforts always ours,
through the Holy Spirit's wings.
Our burdens lifted through your love,
cause our hearts to sing.

Without you Lord, I just don't know
how our lives would go on.
But with you life is easy Lord,
your love makes us strong.

ANGELS

I'd love to visit with angels.
What an honor that would be.
For God dispatches angels,
to care for you and me.

And though we cannot see them,
we feel their presence here.
And we know somehow a sense of peace,
whenever they are near.

RELIEF

It's hard to wait for answers
when we aren't in control.
But we know that Jesus hears our prayers
from the very depths of our souls.

In His time, not ours is the answer.
So He sends patience and chases the doubt.
But the fears creep in, like a stormy night,
makes us wonder, what this is about.

Then I fall on my knees in submission.
Put my burdens right back in His arms.
And I feel a relief as they're lifted,
as my soul knows I'm safe from all harm.

COMMUNION

Oh Lord, you are so precious in my sight.
I want to be precious in yours.
I look to you to care for me.
Your protection is lavished,
encircling my very being.
I know you care and I rejoice.

I give you my worries, my cares
and I feel them lifted.
Your extended arms,
bearing them heavenward
to defuse with expertise.
Thus, you make the enemy defenseless,
and all is peace.

I praise you and feel joy.
I react in telling others that my heart
abounds in light.
My path is clean and clear,
and you are my reality.

GUIDANCE

Take my hand and I will lead you,
I will give you peace and rest,
in the garden of contentment
where the righteous need no test.
I will give you joy and gladness,
never let you hunger there,
and I'll always be there guiding,
to that place forever fair.

THE MESSAGE

I woke up in the morning
and a song burst from my heart.
I knew God had a message
He wanted to impart.

He said, I love you dearly
and I know you love me too.
He then proceeded gently
to tell me what to do.

Break down the walls of darkness.
Throw open wide the door.
Let people feel the sunshine,
shedding guilt forever more.

There is a new life that I offer
for each and every one.
It's the plan of the redemption
and it's why I sent my son.

Now come, lay down the burdens.
Feel relief from your heavy load.
Put on the garment of praise for me.
walk down contentment road.

Come face to face with Jesus.
He'll lead you all the way,
on paths of righteousness and love
until your final day.

THE CONSOLER

Ever wonder why a friend comes by
just when you need them most?
Or why a problem solves itself?
It's not for us to boast.

It shows our Heavenly Father's love
more perfect than the sun.
He works and everything reacts
for each and everyone.

His Strength

Precious Lord, my faith is cemented.
When I ask, I feel the strength you send.
My fears are suddenly diminished
and I know that once again your ear I bend.

When I sing of you, my heart is lifted
as the Holy Spirit fills my soul.
When troubles come I turn to you Lord,
you change my life and make me whole.

What would I ever do without you?
How could I face the light of day?
You make my life a joy to live, Lord,
help me to walk in your sweet way.

THE UNIVERSE

The stars, the sun, the moon,
God set them all in place,
to give the warmth and peaceful rest
for the whole human race.

Stars help us find directions,
the moon guide oceans too—
the rain and sun keep taking turns
deciding what we'll do.

The clouds too have a purpose,
but sometimes skies are blue.
We never know the future,
just trust—for God loves you!

THE WAITING ROOM

There's joy in meeting new faces,
and a pleasure to share with them
the facts of our life, and listen to theirs
as we find things common to man.

Then we hope for the best for our neighbor
as we sit in the waiting rooms.
And we're richer for having met them,
seems our name is called too soon.

We pray for complete recovery
for those we love so much
and it helps to share the problems
with those whose lives we touch.

SEASONS

As autumn shows it's colors
along the roads we drive,
it brings to mind how Jesus
is very much alive.

We see His hand in nature
and the seasons in our life,
but we feel His presence with us
taking worry out of strife.

If we compare our lifetime
as with seasons, four in all,
we can see the path He's led us,
looking back from spring to fall.

We sense that winter is coming
as it always does you know,
but our warmth will come from Jesus,
never mind the wind and snow.

WORDS

I paused today to think of
all the foolish things I say,
the words spill out
in such a haphazard way,
once said, can't be changed.

I thought how nice it would be
if our words were like chalk
and the recipient a chalk board.
How I would love to erase
the hurts those words might cause.

Since I know that's not a choice,
I'd better hold my tongue
and use the sense God gave me
I'll think before I speak.

I'll plan to ask my Jesus
to guide my words so only good words
do I say, encouraging, positive things,
words I wouldn't want to erase
bringing His peace, instead of remorse.

FEELINGS

I see the different feelings
played out before my eyes,
as I talk with friends and family,
I hear those feelings rise.

Sometimes these different feelings
give rise to much remorse,
other times there's joy and gladness
just depends upon the source.

Each of us have feelings
may they be for you and me,
of kindness and compassion
it will set the spirit free.

Then joy will spread to others
and the laughter will begin,
as the clouds will turn to sunshine
and the dark thoughts start to dim.

Let's depend on Christ our Savior,
He will lead us through the day
as we turn our feelings *Toward* ~~our~~ Him
He will give peace and guide our way.

FRIENDSHIP

There comes a time when things get heavy,
when we're walking all alone.
Suddenly, a friend comes by
and shares the heavy load.

I remember heavy milk pails
from the days spent on the farm.
When someone shared the handle
Eased the burden from the barn.

Instantly the load is lighter
as we travel side by side,
talking of the past and present
comfort comes as we abide.

Our Awesome God

How you bless me, precious Lord
when you hear my call,
you give me strength from day to day,
you keep me steady, lest I fall.

You heal the sick and make us glad
and strengthen faith askew,
hearts are lifted, abound in love—
yes, you give life anew.

How does your love encircle
everyone on earth?
Seeking every living heart
although we have no worth.

Everything we have is yours
yet we keep hanging on
to things that have no meaning
though we know that's so wrong.

Life can be so easy Lord
if we give each day to you,
to use us as you need us,
what a joy to live for you!

LOVE-LIGHT

Jesus' love is shining
through a mother's heart;
casting glows on children
from the very start.

Teaching them His goodness
through her gentle care;
watching them with kindness
as they crawl each stair.

When the raisings over
and the new life has begun;
then she has more time to pray
for each and every one.

For a mother's love grows stronger,
it's unselfish too, you know;
for the Lord instilled that nature
in the mothers long ago.

THE ANSWER

My child you say you doubt Me
because of hurts in life.
I sent My son to teach you love,
not bitterness from strife.
You say but how could I,
a loving Father do
the things that hurt and hinder
and break my heart in two?

I am a God of love, not fear,
I've brought the good in life.
And all the wrongs are not from Me,
I haven't sent the strife.
Don't put your faith in people
but forgive their foolish ways,
for through forgiveness came My son,
a friend for all your days.

I've sent the sunshine and the rain
and all the things combined.
In every aspect look for good,
you'll see My love entwined.
Give up the fight, I'm waiting
to help you through each day.
I sent My son to die for you,
His love will guide your way.

Lovingly,

Your Heavenly Father

LIFE'S PUZZLE

Our life is like a puzzle
with the pieces all awry.
They finally fit together,
Completed when we die.

The pieces are of all shapes
but form a common bond
to put our world in order
like step-stones cross a pond.

Our friends too are the pieces
to make our lives complete,
to relish and to reminisce
with memories so sweet.

Sometimes we lose the pieces
but their memory lingers on
bringing peace and satisfaction
that somehow makes us strong.

Morning Revere

My friend and his dog went walking
right after break of day.
The birds were singing different songs,
their music seemed to say:

We thank you Lord for sending spring,
we know it's here to stay.
And Joe enjoyed the chorus
as he walked along the way.

He told us how he loved that walk
with awe he praised the Lord
for giving us the gift of peace—
it's nature's great reward.

OBSERVATIONS OF TRUTH

The longer I live, the more I am aware
of God's creative touch.
All nature is impeccably perfect
from Alpha to Omega.

Even our own bodies are more
intricate than any computer.
With awe we recognize through the
Holy Spirit proof that our creator
is the infinity of all.

Lest there be any doubt
that God created,
look upon a new born babe,
a butterfly or a gazelle.
Themselves an example of God's
love, beauty and grace.

REFLECTIONS

The loving things I do and say
reflect the Lord in every way.
The kindly look, a pleasant "Hi",
as I meet a stranger passing by,
just shows that Jesus lives in me.
He washed my soul and set love free.

He gives me joy to pass around,
he tells me when I'm out of bounds.
My Jesus leads from God's own word,
it's truth, the best I've ever heard.
I'm thankful, yes, I'll always be,
that Jesus placed His love in me.

I'm thankful Lord, that I can see,
that it was you upon the tree.
That I'm the sinner not the one
to all those painful things were done.
You give me grace to carry on,
because you loved me all along.

The Promised Rest

When my life on earth is over,
Jesus take me safely home,
where eternal healings given
and no longer need I roam.

Now the darkness overtakes me,
followed soon by heavenly light.
What a glorious awakening,
in His presence, shining white.

When my life on earth is ending,
like a child I come to thee.
All the mysteries I've pondered,
clearly now my soul can see.

The above came to me the exact moment my Mother-in-law, Florence Kuester, died 600 miles away. We were notified of her passing several hours later. She had a stroke and didn't speak 7 years prior to her death.

DEPENDENCY

Oh Lord, how indispensable you are.
I almost slip and fall,
your angels hold me.
You keep my mind fixed to your word.
Your heart overflows with love
and I am safe.

As a wife, mother of six children, grandmother and great-grandmother, the Lord has blessed me with a full, abundant life. I've always loved to write about finding hope and comfort during difficult life experiences and also my own spiritual journey. The words I write are words from the Lord. It's my prayer that these words inspire others to seek a deeper, more personal relationship with the Lord, experiencing the lasting joy and peace that only He can give. I grew up in the 1930s and have seen many changes, but we can all be sure of the Promise—Jesus is the same yesterday, today and forever.

The Journey

By Helen Kuester of Alexandria

As we walk along life's pathway
And the day seems cool and gray
Let us be the ray of sunshine
Be someone's miracle today
Be a giver not a taker
Bless someone dear to you
Help the weary, feed the hungry
God will send the tasks to do
Be a neighbor, be a friend
Have a kind and listening ear
Help solve problems, find solutions
Let them know, the Savior's near

Jan. 2008